What's the Difference?

Turtles and Tortoises

by Lisa M. Herrington

Content Consultant
Dr. Lucy Spelman

Reading Consultant
Jeanne M. Clidas, Ph.D.
Reading Specialist

Children's Press®
An Imprint of Scholastic Inc.

Library of Congress Cataloging-in-Publication Data

Herrington, Lisa M., author.
  Turtles and tortoises / by Lisa M. Herrington.
    pages cm. -- (Rookie read about science. What's the difference?)
    Summary: "Introduces the reader to turtles and tortoises."-- Provided by publisher.
    ISBN 978-0-531-21482-4 (library binding) -- ISBN 978-0-531-21530-2 (pbk.)
  1. Turtles--Miscellanea--Juvenile literature. 2. Testudinidae--Miscellanea--Juvenile
literature. 3. Children's questions and answers. I. Title.

  QL666.C5H47 2016
  597.92--dc23   2015017327

Produced by Spooky Cheetah Press
Design by Keith Plechaty

© 2016 by Scholastic Inc.

Printed in China 62

SCHOLASTIC, CHILDREN'S PRESS, ROOKIE READ-ABOUT®, and associated logos
are trademarks and/or registered trademarks of Scholastic Inc.

1 2 3 4 5 6 7 8 9 10 R 25 24 23 22 21 20 19 18 17 16

Photographs ©: cover left: georgesanker.com/Alamy Images; cover right: Mike
Johnson/Alamy Images; 3 top: subin pumsom/Shutterstock, Inc.; 3 bottom: Anneka/
Shutterstock, Inc.; 4 top: Studio-Annika/Thinkstock; 4 bottom: Smileus/Shutterstock,
Inc.; 7 top: Studio-Annika/Thinkstock; 7 bottom: Smileus/Shutterstock, Inc.; 8 top:
Minden Pictures/Superstock, Inc.; 8 bottom: Isabelle Kuehn/Shutterstock, Inc.; 11:
Andrzej Grzegprczyk/Shutterstock, Inc.; 12: Wirepec/Thinkstock; 15: Edwin Giesbers/
Minden Pictures; 16: Jurgen Freund/Nature Picture Library; 19: Danny Alvarez/
Shutterstock, Inc.; 20: Matthew Oldfield, Scubazoo/Science Source; 23: Ingo Arndt/
Nature Picture Library; 24: Ryan M. Bolton/Shutterstock, Inc.; 25 top: Praisaeng/
Shutterstock, Inc.; 25 bottom: Isabelle Kuehn/Shutterstock, Inc.; 26: Minden Pictures/
Superstock, Inc.; 27: EcoPic/Thinkstock; 28 top: Ryan M. Bolton/Shutterstock, Inc.;
28 bottom: Françoise Emily/Alamy Images; 29: Peter Greste/AFP/Getty Images;
30: Minden Pictures/Superstock, Inc.; 31 top: Isabelle Kuehn/Shutterstock, Inc.; 31
center top: Ingo Arndt/Nature Picture Library; 31 center bottom: Minden Pictures/
Superstock, Inc.; 31 bottom: Edwin Giesbers/Minden Pictures.

Map by XNR Productions, Inc.

Table of Contents

4

Which Is Which?

They both have shells. They both move slowly on land. They are **reptiles**, so they have scaly skin. But which is the turtle and which is the tortoise?

Did you guess right? Turtles and tortoises are a lot alike. But they are not exactly the same. There are ways to tell them apart.

FUN FACT!

Turtles and tortoises cannot leave their shells. The shells are part of their bodies.

turtle

shells

feet

tortoise

freshwater turtle
(red-eared slider)

webbed foot

flipper

sea turtle
(hawksbill)

A Big Difference

What is an easy way to tell a turtle from a tortoise? Ask yourself if it swims in the water.

Turtles spend most of their time in water. Freshwater turtles live in lakes, ponds, and rivers. They usually have webbed feet for swimming. Sea turtles live in the ocean. They use their **flippers** to swim.

Tortoises live only on land. They do not have webbed feet or flippers. Their feet are round and big for walking.

FUN FACT!

The Galápagos tortoise is the world's largest tortoise. It can weigh as much as three people!

A tortoise has thick feet.

scutes

When danger is near, many turtles and tortoises hide. They pull their head, tail, and feet into their shell.

Shell Shapes

Turtles and tortoises are the only reptiles with shells. Their shells are made of bone. Most are covered in hard plates called **scutes**. But look closely! The shells of turtles and tortoises are different.

Turtles have thin, lightweight shells. That helps them swim fast. Their shells can be flat or curved.

Many tortoise shells are high and rounded. Tortoises have thicker shells than turtles. Their shells are heavy. That is one reason why tortoises move slowly.

FUN FACT!

How slow do tortoises go? It takes some tortoises about five hours to walk 1 mile (1.6 kilometers). A person can walk the same distance in about 20 minutes.

The leopard tortoise lives in Africa.

Time to Eat!

Turtles and tortoises both have a strong sense of smell. That helps them sniff out plants to eat.

Turtles also eat small animals. They often feed on fish, snails, grasses, insects, and worms. Sea turtles catch crabs, clams, jellyfish, and other sea creatures.

This green sea turtle is eating a jellyfish.

Tortoises mostly eat plants. They move too slowly to catch other animals. A tortoise may eat grass, shrubs, and even cactus.

FUN FACT!

Turtles and tortoises do not have teeth. Their sharp jaws are shaped like a bird's beak. They use the beak to bite their food.

Galápagos tortoise

Bringing Up Babies

Turtles and tortoises start their lives in eggs. Females dig a hole on land to lay their eggs. They cover their nests and leave them.

After they **hatch**, some kinds of baby turtles head to the water. They must survive on their own.

Leatherback turtles head for the sea right after hatching.

Baby tortoises stay on land. Like turtles, they must learn to live on their own right away.

Some turtles can live up to 80 years. Tortoises live more than 100 years.

Now you know the difference between these animal look-alikes!

FUN FACT!

Some turtles and tortoises lay up to 200 eggs at one time.

tortoise

Turtles and Tortoises

Turtles and tortoises live around the world except in very cold places. Turtles can be found anywhere wet— from backyard streams to oceans. Many tortoises live in hot, dry places.

North America

South America

The **spiny softshell turtle** is one of the largest freshwater turtles in North America. It has a long, pointed snout (or nose).

MAP KEY

Range of turtles and tortoises

Range of sea turtles

Around the World

Europe

Asia

Africa

You can see how the **Indian star tortoise** got its name. It has a star pattern on its shell.

Australia

The **green sea turtle** can be found in warm waters around the world. It can stay underwater for up to five hours!

Antarctica

lives in water and on land

thin, lightweight shell

webbed feet (sea turtles have flippers)

freshwater turtle

Difference?

high, rounded, heavy shell

lives only on land

strong legs and feet

tortoise

The tip of a snapping turtle's tongue is red and is shaped like a worm. When a fish comes in for a closer look, the turtle chomps it up!

The tip of a snapping turtle's tongue is red and is shaped like a worm. When a fish comes in for a closer look, the turtle chomps it up!

The leatherback is the biggest turtle in the world. It can grow to more than 8 feet (2.4 meters) long. This sea turtle is also the fastest swimmer.